WHY GIVE? ANTHOLOGY

A Collection of Essays & Poetry on Giving

I0549012

Compiled & Edited by

JILL-CAPRI SIMMS

WHY GIVE? ANTHOLOGY

A Collection of Essays & Poetry on Giving

Compiled & Edited by

JILL-CAPRI SIMMS

Plumb Line Consulting, LLC

WHY GIVE? ANTHOLOGY

A Collection of Essays & Poetry on Giving

Copyright © 2018 by Jill-Capri Simms

ISBN- 13: 978-0692097991

ISBN- 10: 0692097996

Published by:

Plumb Line Consulting, LLC

Windermere, FL

info@plumblineconsultinghr.com

www.plumblineconsultinghr.com

Printed in the United States.

CONTENTS

PREFACE 1

MARITZA AROCHO-MACDONALD 7

RUTH BASKERVILLE 11

GWEN BENNETT 15

NANCY BERGERON 17

WILLIAM CHERRY 21

SUSAN CLABAUGH 23

ADIEN DIAZ 25

JEMAL FARRELL 27

LENA FORD 31

AISHA HIGHTOWER-HALL 33

MARLENE HOENIG 37

FRANKIE "VERSATIVITY' JOHNSON 39

TEATRA JOSEPH 43

STEPHEN LANGE 49

RUBY MABRY 53

VERONICA NEALY MORRIS 55

CONSTANCE POITIER 59

DEBRA REED 63

FAYE SAXON HORTON 65

DALE SLONGWHITE 67

AUDREY SWIATOCHA 71

NOLA WILLIAMS 75

OTIS WINDHAM 79

ABOUT THE WRITERS 83

ABOUT THE EDITOR 93

PREFACE

I have many favorite adages, but one that is crème de la crème for my life is "If you can do good, do it!" Funny thing, I thought I invented it, but only in my adult years did I discover it's actually a Biblical scripture found in Proverbs 3:27. There's nearly 60 different versions of the English Bible, and in scanning through several -- for comparison sake (noted below) -- I felt aligned with the Word of God; that when you knowingly have the ability to help someone by giving, just do it:

- Do not keep good from those who should have it, when it is in your power to do it. [NLV]

- *Do not withhold good from those who deserve it when it's in your power to help them. [NLT]*

- *Whenever you are able, do good to people who need help. [NCV]*

- *Never walk away from someone who deserves help; your hand is God's hand for that person. Don't tell your neighbor "Maybe some other time" or "Try me tomorrow" when the money's right there in your pocket. Don't figure ways of taking advantage of your neighbor when he's sitting there trusting and unsuspecting. [MSG]*

In late-2017 while attending a Sunday service at Orlando, Florida's Church in the Son, Senior Pastor Alex Clattenburg delivered a simple yet profound message on giving. It's common knowledge that at year-end, Americans rev up and get in the festive "mood" of giving. Yet, what takes place throughout the year? At least one-third of the world's population believe that God

1

gave His only and very best, but why? It's clearly stated in the Bible it was because the omnicient, omni-potent Heavenly Father loved every being on the earth so very much, that He gave His very best...His son Jesus Christ.

Whether it's giving of financial resources, time, talent or wisdom what's the on-going purpose or motive for humankind to give? I could likely conjure up 100 or more of my own opinions, make a host of presumptions, or even Google and discover the psychology behind giving. However, in rather short order I decided to inquire of others. And ask I did by coordinating an essay contest on the "Why Give?" topic. The contest rules were drawn up, a panel of literary judges were organized, and cash prize awards were determined for three overall winners. I was confident the reasoning behind giving would be plentiful and decided to compile the winning and finalist essays into the "Why Give?" anthology.

In 50-plus years I have observed many acts of generous giving, deliberate giving, conditional giving, and even constrained giving. Unequivocally, it can be said that the "act" of giving "should" be a liberating and peaceful experience. But I began pondering whether experiencing liberating and peaceful feelings toward giving is intuitive or instinctual in human beings. [Yes, this is where I got a little deep.]

Is giving intuitive? Meaning, *understanding or knowing without conscious recourse to thought, observation or reason. Or, is giving instinctual? Whereby a set of behaviors that are both unlearned and set in motion as the result of some environmental trigger.* I would surmise that when either intuition or instinct are in effect, the "act" of giving does not demand hyper-analysis, intensified reasoning, or scholastic advancement. Giving is simply done. A need either overtly or covertly presents itself, and like a homing

2

pigeon, givers are attracted and respond to the "needy" situation – again, whether the need is obvious or concealed.

Ironically, although the need may present itself, the act of giving could still be intercepted, disrupted and aborted. Suppose a need is displayed (in any fashion: monetary, comfort, information, reassurance, guidance, support) and in lightning speed the intuitive whisper of "since you can do good, do it" is heard. But what do you do when just as quickly the internal voice of intellect (or perhaps an external voice of reasoning) sounds an alarm? That voice of doing-good could squelch the action of giving from being fulfilled.

For instance, a smile on the face of an always savvy business person, might try to belie what their eyes, aura, and body language cannot. The intuition of a colleague may register that this person internally feels like crumbling. The colleague can derail the opportunity to give by ignoring what their intuition told them and allow, their intellect to take over, by concluding, "They're smart enough to ask if they want my time," or "Everyone has a bad day," or even "They likely have a high-priced therapist to share their woes with, let me just keep my mouth shut." These and a myriad of rational explanations could kick in and over-ride the do-go opportunity.

Conversely, in a swift yet subtle act, the intuitive giver may say to his colleague, "Today let's do lunch at 11:30 a.m. I need to ask you something." That request to do lunch, might simply be an offer of time to give and enable the professional business person talk, share, vent. The colleague has done good!

In yet another scenario, perhaps you're about 10 yards from the entrance to Publix Supermarket. You can see several elementary school-aged Girl Scouts are hawking their cookies. You notice it's high noon, the girls are fidgety and shoppers are avoiding eye contact and passing them by. You know the routine. Your child was a Girl Scout. You instinctively open your wallet and notice you only have a single dollar bill – five times less than the GS Cookie price tag for a single box of cookies. By this time the automatic doors open and you're now in Publix. Once inside, you begin shopping, your brain kicks in and you remember you've committed to significantly reducing your sugar and carb intake. It's all about the healthy eating lifestyle change you've made for the New Year. You complete your shopping of fresh fruits and vegetables, Beyond Burger's Beast Burger, Uncle Ben's Brown Rice, and Whole Wheat Pita Bread. You pay the cashier with your SunTrust debit card.

While exiting the Publix you see Scouts again and know if you purchase one box of Caramel deLites, you'll need to get two. You once again reach for your wallet. That single dollar bill and one thin dime is all the cash you have. You let the girls know although you cannot buy a box of cookies, you'll make a $1.10 donation. The girls jump up and down. They've received cash for their cause. No huge feat, just your instincts of taking action to give. You've done good!

So in my curiosity about giving, the answers to "Why Give?" proved to be interesting and stylistically diverse. Yet, there was a common theme that giving is a good thing; so much so it makes you feel good. My hope is readers of this anthology will become pensive about the topic, find joy in the literary expressions offered, and perhaps conduct an internal examination of whether for them giving is intuitive, instinctual, a combination of both, or entirely something else. Whatever the motivation, may the objective be just to do good. Enjoy.

- Jill-Capri Simms

MARITZA AROCHO-MACDONALD
[Contest Finalist]

At one point in my Why give? I give because it makes daily life worth living. My uncle Pete says, "Yesterday is gone. Live for today! I can't tell you what tomorrow brings, because it's not here." My dad was always positive. His mantra was, "You work with what you have. Make decisions and enjoy life!"

I've found that my father and uncle's simple life mottos have kept me energized for everyday living. As a result, my primary life motto is "give love and laugh!" When giving from the heart I truly don't believe anyone can go wrong. And giving certainly does not always need to be in monetary form. Giving a kind word, a positive gesture, or an action during an ordinary day might be just what they need. And it's so very easy to do! Even giving by investing time in listening to someone vent could be an invaluable gift. Observing someone's body language or facial expression, and responding and giving at the right time could make someone's day.

My co-worker Carol and I were talking about the recent death of another colleague who passed   due to cancer. Carol shared that she had still not fully recovered from the death of another company employee (James) who passed nearly 10 years ago. Carol explained that James' favorite color was red and she decided to wear a red blazer to his wake. However, to her disappointment his family members and friends did not respond favorably to her wearing her red jacket. The memory of the displeased wake attendees had an adverse impact that had lasted nearly a decade. Carol explained she simply could not shake the negative memory. I encouraged her to take another perspective and not replay the event from a negative viewpoint. Instead, remember the red blazer as a signal -- a bon voyage of sorts -- and that she and James would meet again in heaven. The passing of a loved one should always be considered a celebration of life, a new beginning, a journey of faith. Carol's countenance lifted and brightened. She became elated and actually released a sigh of relief. I certainly could have commiserated with her and even took verbal jabs at the poor social etiquette of James' friends and family members. But why waste time? We need to live for today!

Several months ago while in preparation for Hurricane Irma I was at the supermarket check-out and noticed the cashier had a few bags of groceries sitting on the counter. A young lady was standing nearby and looking somewhat anxious. I wanted to ensure my groceries did not get mixed in with the bagged groceries, and the cashier advised me the young woman was awaiting her brother's arrival because she didn't have enough money to cover the bill – she was $43.00 short. I advised the cashier to add the $43.00 to my bill. However, the young woman said her brother was on the way. Yet, I could detect concern in her young eyes. There were five other people waiting in our same check-out line that seemed agitated. I advised the young woman that I wanted to bless her by covering her bill, and that one day she would have the opportunity to pay it forward for someone as well. The cashier and several people in line in unison said, "God bless you!" I'm not sharing this story for applause, however sometimes when your heart and mind meet to give, go for it! Sometimes you don't know what another person needs, but sometimes you absolutely do know. And when it's within your power to do something about it, do it!

There is a song called, "Christmas Shoes". I encourage everyone to listen to it. It will change your life. The lyrics explain that small things do matter. I have had situations in my upbringing that could have caused me to continuously look back and be stuck. These negative events were not easy to get over; actually they've taken me some years to let go. However, with my mantra being "live, love and laugh" I've realized the ultimate feeling and action of importance is love. I'm a realist. I am not perfect and I have my flaws. However, I've chosen to look beyond my past and focus on love. And when you're giving love to yourself and others on a daily basis, you're winning!

Recently, an agency employee was offered permanent employment with my company. It had been a year in the making. For nearly a full 12 months I provided her training and encouragement. I observed and appreciated her commitment to her work and the job. Upon notification of her permanent job offer, she emailed me to express her appreciation. Her words were filled with enthusiasm. She said, "Thank you for the opportunity you gave me almost a year ago. I appreciate everything you taught me, and the time you spent training me." I responded to her email, "I am proud of you. I love your patience and attitude. You're a wonderful young lady!" Her response, "OMG! Thank you so much for these words. If it weren't for you I would not have had the opportunity. This is the best Christmas present I could receive!"

You never know how you can be a blessing to someone. On a daily basis treat people how you want to be treated. Smile and say "hello". Be encouraging. Show respect for the elderly. I love to address them as young man or young lady...although they may actually be in their 80's, 90's, or even older. Appreciate waking up each morning and thanking God for the day, because tomorrow is not promised. Give because it's the best way to live, love and laugh every single day.

RUTH BASKERVILLE

[Contest Judge]

I grew up respecting givers, having been taught to send a written thank-you note before I could enjoy the gift. However, I quickly learned that the feeling I got from giving exceeded the joy I felt receiving. Since I love and live by the Word of God, let me offer biblically rooted reasons to answer the question, "Why Give?".

In Genesis 8:22, God assures us, "While the earth remaineth, seedtime and harvest, and cold and heat, and summer and winter, and day and night shall not cease." God thought giving in the form of planting seeds, and reaping the resulting harvest, are as important as the weather, the seasons and the light and darkness. We've all heard the expression that we reap what we sow. I can attest to the fact that we reap more than we sow when our thanks comes from God and not man.

I give thoughtful gifts on special occasions, and to be sure I don't miss any of these, I keep a calendar of important dates for the people I love. I study their habits and purposefully choose gifts that will make them smile. I never count the number or kind of gifts that come back to me because I don't have a single day without receiving a blessing that gives me reason to smile. That's why I give!

I also give because my mind and heart are open to the needs of others. God says if we take care of the least powerful people, we're taking care of God Himself. We pass by neighbors, co-workers, organization members, and even family and friends daily, usually asking the rhetorical question, *"How are you doing?"* All we really want to hear back is, *"Fine, great and dandy!"* I've learned that if I ask the question out of a sincere heart, people will volunteer something about their needs. If I'm able to fulfill a need, I will. If not, I'll secure a necessary resource to help the situation. That's why I give!

I believe that intangible gifts are as important as tangible ones. The *Holy Bible* speaks to us giving our "time, talent and treasure." I don't always have financial resources available, but I find immense value in giving of my time. Most of us want someone to listen to us, without judgment. We want friendships free from gossip and disingenuous words of caring. All of us can find time to give of ourselves, regardless of how busy our calendar says we are.

What about talent? Many of us recall learning in Sunday school about the master of the house giving five talents to one servant, two to another, and one to a third. When he asked for an account, the first two had doubled their investments, but the third hid his one talent. For not understanding the Principle of Seedtime and Harvest, and wasting the talent God had put inside him before he was born, he was severely punished.

The take-away is that each of us has unique talents, or things that come easily to us. I believe it's up to us to share that which comes easy to us because we will surely need someone else to share what we struggle to complete. We give of our talents because they were not given to us to hoard or hide. Like gifts of time and treasure, talent is every bit as important to share with others. That's why I give!

Finally, I have come to delight in planting seeds whose harvest is delayed while I work on being patient and humble – and grateful for what I don't see. We're a society built on receiving immediate gratification from every little thing we do, and we're willing to plant seeds if we can reap an immediate harvest. However, just like the birthing cycle takes nine months, seedtime and harvest are not interconnected in the immediacy of time. They are, however, most definitely interconnected! Seeds need watering and nurturing, good soil and nutrients, and precious time to bring forth the bountiful harvest of crops.

Over the years, I've struggled to master the art of patience, more than humility and gratitude. But I've finally grasped the idea that waiting in anticipation of my harvest is not being idle. It's keeping my "eyes on the prize" until I realize that prize. It's always worth the wait! And that's why I give!

GWEN BENNETT

[Contest First Place Winner]

When the question is asked "Why give?" my immediate bounce back is "Why live?"

Part of my personal philosophy is we are on this earth to serve each other, to be the arms and legs of God. There are so many ways to give and there is no tangible value on any act of kindness. I wrote a poem, five years ago titled "Service" and to paraphrase it, I wrote: *Give a Dollar, Give a Dinner, Give a Ride, Give a Smile, which is more valuable?...Just Serve.*

As long as one gives with an open heart and feels that you're being an instrument of God, it has more value than you will ever know.

Case in point, I was serving as a missionary leader for my church many years ago and hosted many young people from all over the world, who took two years of their young adulthood to go to different states and countries to serve. I took the assignment as a form of my giving to help others, only to find that it was the most rewarding experience of my lifetime. I was able to share and serve as an Ambassador to several young people who had not been in personal communications with people of color. At the beginning of their assignments, some really didn't understand that we are all the same...human beings, with the same emotional desires and temporal needs. This awakening was their reward for their service.

We had weekly meetings where they would report their activities. In this process, I met a young female missionary from Australia who told me a story of her interface with a young black man, with long unkempt dreads, in a rural area of Belle Glade, Florida. This is a town where farm labor and low pay is the norm, a hard way of living. Every day she would position herself near the lunch area and speak to him, asking if he wanted to take lessons on the teaching of Jesus Christ and he would just walk by her looking very dejected and depressed. Her first reaction was a feeling of rejection, but she shook it off and let her heart be her guide and continued to be steadfast in her offer of hope.

One day, he finally stopped and began to talk with a hint of a West Indian accent and politely said: "Thank you". She replied, "You are welcome, but what are you thanking me for?"

He replied that he was very depressed lately because his wife had died in childbirth along with the baby, which left him alone in a strange new country. He admitted he was on the brink of killing himself and the one thing that kept him from committing suicide was his reflecting back on her heartfelt smile and hope she gave to him each time he walked past her.

Need I say more? Do you see why it doesn't matter what you "Give"? It matters that you give with a complete sincerity and love.

Because love is the answer, I give you this story for a value unknown.

NANCY BERGERON

[Contest Finalist]

What a daunting question! From the earliest memories of my childhood I heard the quote from Jesus, "It is more blessed to give then receive" (Acts 20:35). Of course, as a child, this message did not resonate well for my focus was on receiving my own coveted toy or doll under the Christmas tree. As a teenager, I was too inward focused to consider the needs of others because I was overcome with the "me, myself and I" stage of my development.

Later I was married and considered an adult, living with someone who had wants and needs of his own. Together we had dreams and goals for our future and the rest of the world was outside of our peripheral vision. When our daughter arrived, our focus shifted to the needs and multiple desires of our little girl. Not to say that we didn't give but giving was a small part of our struggling budget and time.

As I grew more comfortable with my adulthood I noticed that life was not as generous to some as it was to us. I often complained of "why me?" whenever there was a minor crisis or an obstacle on my life's path that I felt was undeserved. Of course, no one else had the "monumental problems" that I had to deal with but I did start to recognize that the life I led was one of privilege; that I was surrounded by love and that I was safe. I wondered what I could do to help others not so blessed; I wondered what the purpose of my life should be and, more importantly, what should I be doing to help those less fortunate.

How come I am so blessed in my life but never quite satisfied? Was it truly more blessed to give than receive? Sister Teresa was quoted as saying "This is the meaning of love, to give until it hurts". She was a true example of a life well lived. How much was I willing to give or sacrifice? "For it is in giving that we receive", says Frances of Assisi. "Do all the good you can, by all the means you can, in all the ways you can, in all the places you can, at all the times you can, to all the people you can, as long as ever you can," thus says John Wesley. Inspired by the examples of others and my mission based church, I began to shift my focus from receiving to giving.

The biggest shift in my philosophy regarding giving took place on a mission trip with our church youth group. We flew to Nuevo Laredo, Mexico to assist in the building of a church at a new colonia (neighborhood). We were greeted by families that lived in dirt floor huts. There was even a family living in a bus. These people had come to the border of Mexico and the United States, perhaps to find a way to cross the Rio Grande to the life of bounty they could visually see across the river. Whatever the reason, they had squatted on farm land to try to build a permanent community. The farmer gave up the land to the government and the squatters paid the government to stay. The colonia had a water tower and an "Aqua" truck driving through the colonia delivering water. There would be no more utilities available for quite a while.

Mapy, a woman with a unique history, greeted us. She had the only Banyo (outhouse) available for our use. Mapy greeted us in her wheelchair and invited us into her one room, sparsely furnished, dirt floor home. She didn't speak a word of English but her smile lit up the room. Each morning, we could count on that beautiful smile to encourage us as we worked in the Mexican sun, over 100 degrees each day. We dug a Banyo, cleared the land, (using only hand tools), poured a cement floor for the church and strung barbed wire fencing.

As we worked Noe, our Mexican liaison, told us Mapy's story. She had been in a fatal automobile accident years ago where eight of her family members were killed. She was taken to the morgue, along with the other family members, but after three days she awoke to the surprise of all. She was removed to a hospital where it was determined she was paralyzed from the waist down. She had been married but her husband recently left her on her own and with the aid of the neighbors living in the bus, she was able to stay in her home. This was the story behind this woman with the deep faith, generous heart and beautiful smile.

I remember thinking, "how dare I ever feel sorry for myself ever again" and "how does Mapy have such a strong and powerful faith"? I was not the only one affected by her story and the experience of meeting such materially poor individuals with such deep, and profound faith. When Noe asked if our team would be willing to extend our stay another ½ day to pour a cement floor in Mapy's home our teens stepped up. The adults allowed the youth to vote - give up an afternoon in San Antonio or fulfill this request. There was no hesitation. The floor was poured for a very grateful Mapy and we all took pleasure in knowing that during the next raining season Mapy would no longer struggle to maneuver in her wheelchair.

Why Give? I can only answer for myself. I give because I know in my heart that this is what God wants of me - of us - and the warmth and love I feel in my heart. When I give to help another is the greatest gift I have ever experienced. Yes, "It is more blessed to give then receive". Yes! It truly is!

WILLIAM CHERRY
[Contributing Guest]

The Philippian Church was the only church to give monetary support to Paul's ministry after he left the Greek State of Macedonia of which Philippi was the capital. Paul, describing the history and giving of the Philippian Church in support of his ministry reminds them in Philippians 4: 15: "...when I set out from Macedonia, not one church shared with me in the matter of giving and receiving, except you only;..." [NIV] In verse 16 he adds: "for even when I was in Thessalonica, you sent me aid again and again when I was in need."

Paul knew what it was to be in need, and he promises the Philippian Church, "My God shall supply all your need according to His riches in glory by Christ Jesus." We must always remember there is a big difference between our wants and our needs. A need is something that is essential, something that is indispensable, and something that you and I must have in order to live. Food, water, shelter, clothing, and transportation are things we all need in life. We must have them in order to survive. A want is something I would like to have, something I may wish or long for, something that I find desirable, but it is not something that I must absolutely have. I can live without having all my wants supplied, but all my needs these must be met. God does not promise to supply all our wants, but He does promise to supply all our needs.

Paul rejoices because the generous giving of the Philippian Church to support his ministry has met his needs. He shares in Philippians 4:18 [NIV]: "I have received full payment and even more; I am amply supplied, now that I have received from Ephaphroditus the gift you sent." Then he acknowledges that their gifts are "a fragrant offering, an acceptable sacrifice, pleasing to God." God was well-pleased that the Philippians had given generously to

Paul's ministry and met his needs. Because of their generosity, Paul can reassure them, "And my God shall supply all your needs according to His riches in glory by Christ Jesus."

One lesson I have learned is the fact that you can never out-give God. When you put Him first in all you do in giving. Let me summarize this essay with this: We individually and collectively can receive the same promise/blessing as the Philippian Church was given the promise 'My God shall supply all your need according to His riches in glory by Christ Jesus'. This occurs when we have a generous heart in giving to God.

SUSAN CLABAUGH

[Contest Finalist]

I love to give. It fills a place inside me when I give. For many years I thought this was a good attribute. God said, "It is more blessed to give than receive." I figured how could I go wrong when God says it's right. However, I was going very wrong.

When I gave to someone: cards, gift cards, needed money, special gifts, just because; I gave with a secret hope. A hope I would receive something in return. Their acceptance, love, friendship, time, a gift back to me, or even just a card back to me showing they care too. It never worked. I did not receive those things. It took me years of giving like this to realize what I was doing wrong.

First, for several years, I didn't have the resources to be giving the way I was giving. God says to be good stewards of our money and I was going into debt at times to buy things for people just to get them to like me or show me their love and acceptance. I felt they would think less of me if I didn't give them things, yet they gave me nothing in return, so my thought process was messed up.

I grew up thinking giving is how you show your love. Gifts abounded in my childhood and teenage years. If I won an award or did a good job on my report card, a gift or money was given to me; instead of the simple love I much desired.

I learned my habits from this time, and I thought it was how you show love. I also was using giving to avoid recognizing in myself what I needed to deal with about my past. The abuse and assaults.

As long as I concentrated on others and doing things for them, then I didn't have time to focus on dealing with the memories and horrible things coming up about my past. I could instead put my attention on other people.

God does not want this for us. He does not want us to give or do out of obligation, or to gain love, friendship, favor, or to fill a void. He wants us to give, but out of the true spirit of giving.

Since realizing this I have begun to pray about my giving. Praying for God to lead me where I should give, or to whom I should give and when. It may be money, a card, things, time, or love. Giving like this brings a joy which knows no bounds. It also allows God to fill my void with Him instead of material things or other people.

Giving to people when God directs us to and not to cover our pain, but to give in the spirit of giving. This is the lesson God taught me this past year. One I continue to learn each and every day.

Why do I give? To show the love of my God.

ADIEN DIAZ

[Contest Finalist]

Giving is an act of selflessness. A person does not need to be financially or materially rich in order to provide a way to fulfill a need. People who give are driven by a heart of compassion, love, and mercy. They give generously, ungrudgingly, and without seeking reward. Throughout the year many days are set aside to observe or promote the act of giving, such as Humanitarian Day, International Day of Charity, World Kindness Day, National Philanthropy Day, Giving Tuesday and International Volunteer Day. However, no matter what day you choose, any day is good to extend a helping hand and donate resources or time to someone in need.

There are many opportunities to give, but often we struggle because we don't know where to start, where to give, or who to give to. What matters the most is that we take action, develop a plan, and invite others to join us in giving. Giving is an act of worship; positioning ourselves before God and expressing our gratitude for all that He has done for us. This magnifies the trust we place in Him for our future.

As we prepare ourselves to give an examination of the heart must be in place; remembering all the blessings that have been given to us. In turn, we supply our many talents so we can be His hands and feet here on earth. We should not focus on seeking a reward or recognition for our acts, or ask God to look at us differently because we are giving. When we give our hearts must be filled with joy. When we give, we should willingly and sacrificially give. This is imitating God, by answering a call to a need. As a result, we create a chain of continuous generous giving by donating what we have, without neglecting our own personal necessities, family, and financial responsibilities.

Being in the ministry of giving will increase our thankfulness to God Our Provider; understanding that receiving a blessing is a way for us to be enriched in every aspect of our lives. Giving makes a way to provide the necessities within our communities, place of work, church, and neighborhood. As we receive these increases our hearts turn toward gratefulness and thanksgiving by following the example of our Lord and Savior Jesus Christ. This brings all the glory to God, by acting in obedience and remembering where our help truly comes from.

God loves the poor and this is why we are entrusted with much, not only for us to live day-to-day, but to share with others. This is why God has commanded us to give, not only what is due back to Him, but to feed the hungry, clothe the naked, visit the sick, and pray for the needs of others. When we place those needs ahead of our wants slowly we can start finding happiness and joy while our heart is in constant gratification. It is our responsibility to not neglect the poor.

As we prepare to give, let's remember that God is able to meet the need; that a giving and willing attitude is more valuable than any amount of money or time. Don not think what we are giving is too small or too large, because God sees our intention and willingness to give. The reward of giving is not instant gratification, it is the internal spiritual growth that we develop when we meet the needs of others.

JEMAL FARRELL
[Contributing Guest]

Let's look at why we should give and the purpose of it. Giving is a method that enables us to make a connection to each other. The connection between man and the Father was Him giving Himself for us. He gave us a substance of Himself when he blew His breath of life into mankind, so that we might live. Giving always fulfills a greater purpose. Giving should always carry life.

Why did the Father "give"? He gave simply because of His Love. He gave from out of Himself, so we might experience Him! It's important we see the connection between the two so that we will understand the purpose of giving. Let's look at a very familiar scripture: John 3:16 "For God so loved the world that He gave..." Giving is the evidence of God's Love. To give is to love. There is no separation. Love is always the platform that we give from, which is the requirement!

What does giving require? Giving requires surrendering. Messiah is the perfect example. The love He has for the Father enabled Him to give Himself away. Giving always requires us to love beyond ourselves. John 15:13 reminds us, "Greater love has no one than this, that one lay down his life for his friends." What you give the same measure you will receive. I love to say HOW you give determines the same measure you will also receive. The greater the measure of love, the greater the measure of the gift in return. Luke 6:38 says, "Give, and it will be given to you. They will pour into your lap a good measure—pressed down, shaken together, and running over [with no space left for more]. For with the standard of measurement you use [when you do good to others], it will be measured to you in return."

Giving is never selfish nor does it look for anything in return.

27

When we give for the wrong reasons, it's not in the purity of love. When we look for a return, it's the wrong motive. We never give in order to get; that's lust. Why would I say that? Because lust always wants, yet it's never satisfied. Love continues to give! It's always pouring. Our love should also extend to our enemies. As it is stated in Luke 6:35, "But love your enemies, do good, and lend, hoping for nothing in return; and your reward will be great, and you will be sons of the Most High. For He is kind to the unthankful and evil."

Let's address another part of giving. Giving is intended for the receiver to embrace the love that's transpiring in the giving from the giver. For example, because I love you, my action of love is shown in my giving. I'm giving simply out of love because of love. No motives. No wrong desires. Just love! Our love should be as unconditional as our giving, just as the Father's love is unconditional towards us. This is another reason we don't look for a return. When we do, we have just put a condition on our giving.

We view money as our biggest part in giving where love should be. Money is a currency we exchange with. Love is also a currency we use to exchange. When we love the currency of money over the currency of love, we fall victim to 1 Timothy 6:10, which states, "The love of money is the root of all evil". It is not the currency (money), but the love of it that's evil. When love is in the wrong place, our desires become corrupt which causes the wrong motives that enables the evil to exist in our hearts. Matthew 6:24 gives proof of this. It says, "No one can serve two masters. For you will hate one and love the other. You will be devoted to one and despise the other. You cannot serve both God and money."

Giving is the evidence of being in love. The world tells us to *Fall in Love* when we are supposed to be *Giving Love*. It's never about falling in love. It's about releasing, growing, and maturing in love.

Falling in love is an expression describing one's emotional state. However, love is not an emotion. It's an act of one's will. Love is not about feelings or emotions, because love can exist apart from feelings. The truth is, no feelings are needed to obey His command to love your neighbor as yourself.

The Hebrew word for love is ahava and the root word of ahava is ahav which means to give. So, when we ask the question *"Why Give?"* we are asking *"Why Love?"* Without truly engaging love we cannot truly experience and begin to understand giving.

LENA FORD

[Contest Third Place Winner]

Why give? Because giving reproduces after its kind.

Inside a fertile womb of a wife, a husband gives seed, and at the appropriate time she gives birth. Both of them now have a baby. It is the law of reciprocity. He gave, she received. In return, she gave, he received. Now both of them are beneficiaries of the gift.

A farmer plants seeds into the ground. But before he plants, he tills the ground. After the seeds are planted, he nurtures and waits with great anticipation for a harvest. Finally, the season has arrived and the farmer rejoices at what he sees. He gave seeds to the ground and the earth gave back to the farmer a harvest that outnumbered what he initially gave to the earth. It's the law of sowing and reaping.

A loved one dies. His or her body has yielded itself to the earth, giving up its mortal body as a seed. In return, it gives the gift of spirit to the loved ones left behind to motivate, build, change, and carry on legacy. It's the law of impartation.

Why give? Because giving releases blessings.

Bring the whole tithe into the storehouse, that there may be food in my house. Test me in this," says the LORD Almighty, "and see if I will not throw open the floodgates of heaven and pour out so much blessing that there will not be room enough to store it (Malachi 3:10 NIV). Many of us may have heard this preached across pulpits. While for some, this might serve as a marketing get-rich-quick scheme, preying on the vulnerabilities of the poor. For others, it is a testing of faith, believing that when we make provisions for those in need in our communities and beyond, an abundance of blessings will attach itself to our cupboards,

31

refrigerators, freezers and pantries, resulting in an overflow of blessings that we cannot contain. Therefore, it becomes the gift that keeps on giving.

A husband died, making his wife a widow. There was no life insurance policy enforced to pay off the mortgage and other expenses. Their sons were about to be sold as slaves. But out of desperation, she asked the Prophet Elisha for help. He asks, "What do you have in your house?" She replied: "I have nothing but a jar of oil." Okay, time to go to work. Go find some investors. Take their borrowed vessels, go home, shut the door, and then pour what you have into each jar. In doing this, the widow was able to sell what she had, pay off her debt with money to spare. We can give to others even when we lack money, by pouring ourselves into the lives of others with words of encouragement. He who refreshes others shall be refreshed (Proverbs 11:25 NIV). When she gave out of her lack, blessings were released into her household. She advanced from poverty to a life of affluence.

Why give? Because giving restores hope.

The woman with an issue of blood gave all she had in hopes of receiving her healing but got nothing in return, so it seems. She could have easily given up after exhausting all of her monetary resources, and who would blame her? Instead, her creative energy kicked in and spoke to her senses that if I do something out of the ordinary, perhaps I could get extraordinary results. Instead of being a spectator she decided to press through the crowds; amidst the naysayers. She pressed until she touched the very essence of the one who could restore hope, when she touched the hem of his garment. That very act of faith released a virtue that would burn up her infirmity. Therefore, she was given new life, new freedom and restored hope. She gave something she couldn't see with her natural eye. She gave her faith.

AISHA HIGHTOWER-HALL

[Contest Finalist]

My first lesson on giving was from Ms. Hill. Ms. Hill was old. Old as Methuselah in my mind. She was always giving advice and helping people. They came from all walks of life, and they trusted her. She was a nurse. She was a single mom, but was always giving to other mothers. She spoke her mind to neighbors, to teachers, or whoever stepped in her midst. I know her well, for Ms. Hill was my mother. I had rushed through the door as I pushed my way pass her and slung myself on the bed.

"What's wrong sugar dumpling?" She asked with that sweet voice of hers. I could hardly talk, but I pushed through the words.

"It's Joan Crawford!"

"What happened? Did you two have a fight?"

"No Mama, she hurt my feelings. I can't believe she treated me so badly. You know how we always share with Joan. You feed her every time she comes here. She plays with all my toys, and when you give me money, I always share with her. But today, she knew I was hungry, but she never shared. She ate right in front of me. And when I went to ride her bike, she told me to not touch it.

Then I picked up the video game, but she didn't want me to touch nothing. So I just sat there watching TV, while she played with her other friend. When she saw I was smiling at the program, she turned it off and told me I couldn't watch it.

And all this time she was eating and I was hungry."

"Baby, why didn't you come home?"

"I was seeing how long she would keep up her stinginess. And what was so bad Mama is she let her other friend play with her video game. That was it! That's when I told her to never mind coming to my house for the rest of her life. So that's why I'm crying. I thought she was my friend."

"Well, let's talk about that." She pulled a chair in front of me, and held both of my hands.

"In order to share, you first must learn to give. And to give you must first learn to love. When you love someone, you naturally want to give to them. Do you love Joan?"

"I did before today."

"Most likely if you loved her yesterday, you love her today. But now you see another side of her. It usually takes a series of misgivings to change that. If you knew one thousand babies, all of them want love. God instilled that in us. But giving is learned. It is a choice. It is not instinctual. You are a giver. You will always be a giver. Do you know what happens to givers? They always receive. But here's the key. When you give, never ever expect to receive from the person you gave to. Sometimes it comes from the same person, but don't count on it. The blessing will come from God. God uses his people. Someone will replace Joan. Never give with expectations. If you do bitterness and unforgiveness will surface. Give from your heart."

"Mama is that old folk's advice or is that Gods word?"

"Girl, I'm not old and that's God's word and his promise to us. Luke 6:38 says to give, and it shall be given unto you, good measure, pressed down. You've read it! God gave his only son, Jesus, so that we may live. What if God had said, "Look at those mean people. I would have never given again!" Even though Joan did not give to you, you must continue to give, otherwise you will miss the blessings of heaven."

Of all my classmates' mothers, Mama was the oldest. She was also, the smartest. She knew her bible verses. Always started them, but told me to look it up. I was twelve then. Today I am blessed to live to sixty-five.

So you ask, "Why give?" Today I would teach my daughter that giving is like a self-serving bank account that will last! Ching! Ching! It will bring joy to your soul. Giving is power. It brings confidence. Giving is like having a double heart in your body. You don't need Christmas because you are always full of glee.

Why give? Giving is manna to the marrow of the bones. Try it! Every year I ask God to increase my tithings, and he does it. Wow! And you can too.

During Stage-4 Breast Cancer, my giving brought hundreds of people to my aid by delivering dinners and gift packages to my children. Employees gave their vacation hours in the form of cash to me. Every Christmas, I invite fifty to seventy people to my home and give each of them three to five presents. My home is so full of furniture and food that I look for people to give to.

Giving is found throughout the world and the bible. It is the foundation for any society. The United States has an Office of Protocol Gift Unit which selects gifts for Presidents of various countries. Giving brought two combating brothers, Isaac and Esau back together. The Shunammite woman's kindness perceived the holy man, Elisha, to her house and she fed him. Be like Zaccheus, who gave his goods to the poor. When you give, you benefit the most, because you know that God has supplied you with abundance.

MARLENE HOENIG

[Contributing Guest]

God's Word is true and it is certain

It divides between the soul, spirit, and life's curtain

It says God holds the keys between temporary and eternal

And separated darkness from the light

He upholds what is truth and what is right

Why give?

Because God gave first

God created life; then gave His life to satisfy sin's thirst

Heaven's door is opened wide for those who will receive

God's Holy gift of eternal life.

Why Give?

Because He gave first

He sent His Son – the Living Word and Eternal King

To show His love for all the world-redeeming everything

Disciples share God's saving plan and how Jesus broke the curse

Why give?

Because God gave His love first.

God is true and He is certain

He never tells a lie

He created the world and He loves you and I

He will never change his mind

We are His love burst

Why give?

Because He gave first.

FRANKIE "VERSATIVITY' JOHNSON

[Contest Second Place Winner]

I've been contemplating this topic "Why Give?"

Thinking too deeply instead of accepting what it really is

It's simply asking why give...

You see I give because it's the right thing to do

I give because I know how it feels walking in those same shoes

I know what it's like not having the money when the bills are due

I know how it feels not having someone to turn to

I know how it feels going to bed without something to eat

Tossing and turning because your stomach is upset not allowing you to sleep

I know how it feels waking up feeling this is the day for change

Reflecting on your situation as the positivity quickly turns to pain

I know how it feels going through the day with your mind somewhere else

Being in that state of loneliness believing all you have is yourself

I know how it feels just wanting someone to hear your voice

To just listen instead of judging saying your situation is your choice

But really you just want to talk

You admire them so you just want them to show you how to walk

Because we have all slipped and came short of the glory

It's some places we've been that we don't mention in our story

Because we've all made mistakes so why do we constantly turn the other cheek?

You see I give because I love and I give because I see

That a change in you could be a gift from me

You see I give because I want to be the change in the world today

I give because it may be someone who has lost their way

I give to be a difference

I give from the heart so my giving doesn't need to be mentioned

I give because that's all I know

I give to not only encourage but to provide hope

I give for that child dealing with abuse in the house

In any of the aspects but is afraid to speak out

I give for that parent trying to provide their for child's needs

But times got hard and circumstances knocked them off their feet

I give for that individual that's serving time

Especially for the one whose sentence doesn't fit the crime

I give for that individual with no roof over their head

Still remaining strong even though they have a piece of cardboard for a bed

I give for that individual who just wants a hot meal

I give for that one that just needs a hug to feel

That warmth and compassion to keep their head up

Provide reassurance they're not alone when the road feels rough

I give because we were all created to serve a purpose

That one could help the other if we knew what our worth is

I give because I've given and I know what it brings

The feeling of genuinely helping someone is what love really means

So give something whether it's time money or love

Because we've all needed someone to lift our spirits up

And that's why they say it's better to give than receive

I'll give all I can for you hoping you would do the same for me

So ask yourself, "Would you give?"

TEATRA JOSEPH

[Contributing Guest]

Would you withhold visuals from a movie?

Would you withhold sound from a noise?

Would you withhold milk from a baby?

Would you withhold oxygen from the lungs?

Would you withhold sunlight from the plants?

Would you withhold from a human being their soul?

Would you withhold water from the springs?

Would you withhold warmth from a heart that has grown cold?

Someone asked, "Why give?" and I respond, "Why withhold?"

For God gave the greatest gift, His son Jesus

Because God loves us so!

Are we greater than the Creator?

No.

So, why give?

Because we can't take anything when we leave this earth

Except our spirit and our soul.

"Me, myself and I" is a selfish and sad way to live life

To keep your hands, heart and mind so closed that you don't realize

The prison you're in

So stop for a moment, look around, can you imagine?

What if the trees that enable us to breathe withheld the oxygen?

Now wouldn't that be something!

Imagine if the sun withheld its light

Imagine if God withheld rain from the sky

Without the water we would die

This is what happens to a person who doesn't give

They slowly dry up inside

You don't have to be wealthy in order to give

Sometimes the most memorable gifts are those that only cost time

And a kind and thoughtful mind

So you smiled at the stranger that passed you on the street

You spoke to the man that everyone else acted like they didn't see

You gave groceries to that family who had little or nothing to eat

You visited that family member who for years you haven't seen

You gave comfort to a friend in their time of need

You complimented someone, who little did you know, had low self-esteem

You encouraged the youth, giving them hope for what lies ahead

You spent time with the elderly letting them know they haven't been forgotten

In you they have a friend

You showed kindness to the one everyone shunned

You gave love to the one everyone else had given up on

God is the greatest example of being a giver, for He's the greatest giver of all

And if it's good enough for Him to give

Why not be good enough, and harken to the call?

Jesus said, *"For I was hungry and you gave me something to eat, I was thirsty and you gave me something to drink, I was a stranger and you invited me in, I needed clothes and you clothed me, I was sick and you looked after me, I was in prison and you came to visit me."*

The Word of God says, "Give and it shall be given unto you."

There is no room for selfishness in this golden rule

When asked, "Why give?"

I respond, "Why withhold?"

You can't take anything with you when we leave this place

Except the Spirit and your soul

There is no way around giving

No matter how hard you try

You can give while you live or you can give when you die

For someone will possess what you once owned, for there is no need for it

In the great "by and by"

You can give while you live

And experience the blessings of having an open heart and open hands

For when your heart and hands are open

You have room to receive again

To live a life of withholding is to die

But to live a life of giving transcends expired time

When the body has grown cold and life has left its fleshly home

You will still live in the mind and heart of someone you have given too

For in their memory will be you

Doing as only you can do

When asked, "Why give?"

I reply with these examples of why

There are a lot of reasons for giving, but you must give

In order to understand and appreciate the whys

STEPHEN LANGE

[Contest Finalist]

God commands us to give generously to other people, to help people in need. When we are generous and give we are reflecting the nature of God that we have abiding in us through the Holy Spirit. We give to others from what God has already given to us. God frees us from a spirit of stinginess and worry over money. We rest in the provision and promise of God.

God is a loving God and that love expresses itself in generosity. God created us and gave us life. When we rejected Him and went our own way, did He give us what we deserved? No, He gave Himself for us, by dying to redeem us. He gave us His love and calls us His friends!

Through our redemption in Christ, God has given us eternal life. Being born again, God has bestowed on us His name and we've been made His sons and daughters. He has given us the treasure of His word! God has given every born again Christian His Holy Spirit who reveals to us all that God has given us.

Not only have we received of God's generosity here and now, but we've been given an everlasting inheritance in Christ, future riches and rewards that can't be counted or imagined. God has made Christ heir of all things. What does Jesus do with His name and His inheritance? He generously shares them with us!

God has given us everything, and when He tells us to give to others He's saying, "Share what I've given you!"

Out of gratitude for God's generosity we give to others. And gratitude to God is always reason enough to be generous. As Christians, our desire is to honor and glorify the Lord in our lives, and showing mercy to others by being generous glorifies Him! The wisdom of the world says, hang on to what you have and keep trying to get more! God says to let go of what you have and He will replenish and increase it.

People who refuse to give are not only ungrateful, but they are showing by their disobedience that they don't believe. When we follow God's commands to give, we are showing by our obedience that we believe the word of God.

There are two different acts of giving that we are called upon to practice. There is the giving of our tithes to the Lord, and there is the giving of gifts and offerings to help others.

Some people say that Christians don't need to tithe, that it is only an Old Testament command. They use the fact that we are not under the law, but under grace for their argument. And in that respect they are right, our salvation is not dependent on our tithing. But tithing is an acknowledgment that what we have come from God. It is an act of faith. We believe God's word that He will make provision for us. We trust God and depend on Him to prosper us, and we tithe.

We give gifts to charitable organizations and to people in need. When choosing an organization to donate money to, we should examine their overhead. How much of the money donated to the organization goes to run it? Salaries and administrative costs make up part of the overhead of a charitable organization. The top charities run on five or ten percent overhead! Pray to God for wisdom in your giving to charitable organizations!

When we think about giving money to individuals, it becomes harder to know what to do. We have to listen to the Holy Spirit and exercise wisdom.

In poor countries, people live on very little, and it's easy to justify giving something to people who ask because we know they have nothing and they need it. In our country, sometimes we're unsure if the person asking us for money is really in need. How do we tell if we should give to people who ask? Should we say no to some people and give to others?

When I gave my life to Christ, I wanted to be generous, but was always suspicious of people asking for money. I came to understand that I was saying no to some people God wanted me to give money to. I overcame my habit of saying no, by trusting God that when I gave money I was really giving it to Him. I didn't have to decide if the person was worthy and deserved the money, or really was in need. I would pray and dedicate the money to God and then I would give it to the person who asked. Praying to God for that person, I trusted God to speak into their hearts, and then gave them money. We are not to judge the motives of people that God tells us to give money to.

There are still people that I say no to when they ask me for money. If I know absolutely that the money is going to buy drugs or alcohol, I refuse. If I know absolutely that the person is lying to me about the reason that they need the money, I refuse. If I don't know absolutely, I give them the benefit of the doubt. I put it in the hands of God and give. God saved us when we didn't deserve it, and His desire is to do the same for others.

When we show mercy and give, we're revealing God's grace to people. When we pray for the people that we give money to, they can't escape from God speaking to them. Perhaps someday they'll come to know the Lord because they saw His grace demonstrated to them through us.

Ask the Lord to give you a generous heart. It will be His delight to do it for you!

RUBY MABRY

[Contest Finalist]

I give because it's selfless.

I give because it makes me feel good to make someone's heart smile.

I give because I was raised to never look down on someone due to their "lack"; because one day that could be me.

I give because I've learned one of the best ways to pick myself up is to give back and pay it forward.

I give not because I have to, but because I want to.

I give because in a world full of negativity it's the positive thing to do.

I give because I may not have "much", but my "much" could be someone's overflow.

I give because growing up as a child I saw and heard (and I've seen, heard and witnessed) people with no food to eat, no place to live, and no clothes on their backs.

I give because my heart aches for anyone who is in need.

I give because I have a caring and compassionate heart that does not have an "off button".

I give because it's an electrifying feeling from my head to my toes.

I give because it was my foundation growing up as a child.

I give because it is rewarding.

I give because it uplifts others.

I give because it's the Christian thing to do.

I give because my parents instilled in me the passion for giving, sharing and loving.

I give because I know no other way.

The best gift of giving is simply giving from the heart. That is giving the best piece of yourself. When we can all learn to give and pay it forward, this world would be such a better place. So many people walk around day in and day out lacking the basic necessities they need to live. It doesn't take much to do a good deed and spread the love by giving. The more you give, the more you get back. Giving is good medicine for the soul. It not only fulfills you, but it fulfills the person being gifted. Some people fall upon hard times and it is very difficult and sometimes simply embarrassing to ask for help. It is important for us to treat others how we want to be treated. A little goes a long way. When giving, no amount is too small. It's the thought that counts.

Doing for others brings a sense of joy and it is a great feeling to know you are changing someone's life for the better. Giving makes the world go 'round. It enriches not only your life but someone else's.

I've learned that it's not what you have, but what you do with what you have. Give from your heart and elevate the world's vibration. Society needs more love and kindness. Do your part and give, give and give.

Always remember that no matter where you are in life, what's going on, what burdens you carry, above ALL, do what's right and good things are bound to happen. Life is reciprocal. Be careful how you treat it.

VERONICA NEALY MORRIS

[Contest Finalist]

Giving, in my humble opinion, is the flip side of receiving. Now I don't think one should give simply to get something back, but at the same time it is a proven truth that those who give will receive in return. Allow me to explain! Think about it. It's virtually impossible to understand giving if you've never been given anything. The *Holy Bible* says, *"Give and it shall be given back to you pressed down, shaken together and running over."* Giving and receiving go hand- in-hand.

Having said that, I believe we should give because the Word of God encourages us to do so, especially for "born again believers" like me.

On a personal note, giving for me is part of who I am, to the point that it's essentially embedded in both my natural DNA and my spiritual DNA. I also believe the old saying, "It's better to give than to receive." I'm a living witness to how a giver feels when giving something meaningful to someone who needs to receive it.

As a Christian woman, I give out of obedience to God, and that simple premise just works for me – every day, every time! I give because it feels right and it is right. I give because I know first-hand what it feels like not to have, and then to be the recipient of something from a generous giver. I give to those who "have" and who "have not." I give because it's a gift that keeps on giving. I give because I understand the spiritual and universal laws that govern giving. Listen, these laws were put in place before the foundation of the world, and there is nothing man can do to change them. In essence, I am wise enough to know that not to give will evoke the "Law of Lack" or the "Law of

Poverty" on my life. That may seem a puzzling concept, but it's accurate.

I give because I like to be in alignment with giving and receiving. I give because I like the mathematics of it; in the sense that the more you give, the more you receive. And it doesn't have to mean you receive from the one to whom you gave. You WILL receive! Giving is so opposite from the way the world thinks, in that it doesn't always make logical sense. It's magical in that oftentimes you don't get it back in the same form that you gave. I even give for what seems like selfishness, which happens when I give because I like the return. God promises to reward givers, and He is especially fond of helping the poor, like widows and orphans.

Finally, I give because it gives me a sense of connection and community; and it makes me feel like I am part of something bigger than myself. I believe I am anointed to give, and by obeying God's commands telling me to whom and when to give, I remain in God's grace.

Giving, in my humble opinion, is the flip side of receiving. Now I don't think one should give simply to get something back, but at the same time it is a proven truth that those who give will receive in return. Allow me to explain! Think about it. It's virtually impossible to understand giving if you've never been given anything. The *Holy Bible* says, *"Give and it shall be given back to you pressed down, shaken together and running over."* Giving and receiving go hand- in-hand.

Having said that, I believe we should give because the Word of God encourages us to do so, especially for "born again believers" like me.

On a personal note, giving for me is part of who I am, to the point that it's essentially embedded in both my natural DNA and my spiritual DNA. I also believe the old saying, "It's better to give than to receive." I'm a living witness to how a giver feels when giving something meaningful to someone who needs to receive it.

As a Christian woman, I give out of obedience to God, and that simple premise just works for me – every day, every time! I give because it feels right and it is right. I give because I know first-hand what it feels like not to have, and then to be the recipient of something from a generous giver. I give to those who "have" and who "have not." I give because it's a gift that keeps on giving. I give because I understand the spiritual and universal laws that govern giving. Listen, these laws were put in place before the foundation of the world, and there is nothing man can do to change them. In essence, I am wise enough to know that not to give will evoke the "Law of Lack" or the "Law of Poverty" on my life. That may seem a puzzling concept, but it's accurate.

I give because I like to be in alignment with giving and receiving. I give because I like the mathematics of it; in the sense that the more you give, the more you receive. And it doesn't have to mean you receive from the one to whom you gave. You WILL receive! Giving is so opposite from the way the world thinks, in that it doesn't always make logical sense. It's magical in that oftentimes you don't get it back in the same form that you gave. I even give for what seems like selfishness, which happens when I give because I like the return. God promises to reward givers, and He is especially fond of helping the poor, like widows and orphans.

Finally, I give because it gives me a sense of connection and community; and it makes me feel like I am part of something bigger than myself. I believe I am anointed to give, and by obeying God's commands telling me to whom and when to give, I remain in God's grace.

CONSTANCE POITIER

[Contest Finalist]

Giving brings out the good in us. The reason we give is because it is in our nature to be a viable component to the human race. Most people want to be on the list of people who are good. Nice people are always friendly, smiling and giving. There is joy associated with giving. Joy is a positive emotion that results from feeling good about what we are doing and for the receiver, what has been done. When we give, our effectiveness as individuals increase because of the realization that we get to be a part of changed lives. This contributes strength toward our maturity and validates purpose driven lives.

We are made in the image of a giver who gave more than we could ever imagine. He gave his son, Jesus, to die on the cross for our benefit even before we knew him. Many of us give to demonstrate our appreciation as a response to the grace that was given to us. We intrinsically encompass a foundation for the same compassion measureable only to the amount we allow ourselves to make personal sacrifices in the interest of meeting the needs of others (many of whom we don't know). As a result, we don't consider it robbery to contribute to organizations, victims in need of relief from natural disasters or becoming knowledgeable of a situation with which we can assist.

As writers, we emulate our creator who wrote to us about his love and desire through letters in the bible. Showing compassion through the pen for those we need to communicate with is one of the ways we know how to share our matters of the heart. We engage in the expression of writing to complete ourselves spiritually, emotionally and physically allowing us to continue developing into the purpose for which we are created.

Giving is two-fold. We are blessed when we are a blessing to others. This is transformed into increased purposefulness when we see the needs of people and contribute to their well-being. It stimulates a joy which sustains our happiness, enriches our spirit and subsequently our overall health. Furthermore, generosity produces the character of human kindness.

Everyone has been given something, howbeit, in different measures, but as noted in the scriptures; "to whom much is given, much is required." "...For unto whomsoever much is given, of him shall be much required..." [Luke 12:48 KJV] When we give much, we receive much in a sense of purpose. Our generous acts are relative to individual circumstances.

Even people in poverty give to those who are more poverty-stricken than they are.

My favorite cliché is "The self is always becoming". We change through each season and experience in our lives. What we give changes based on our personal journeys in life. What I give today is a revelation of what I have come to be based on life's experiences. Our giving can be expressed by identifying with what someone is going through as it relates to our personal experience.

Giving evokes happiness, happiness makes us feel content, and contentment eases the mind. Giving evokes happiness. Happiness makes us feel content. Contentment eases the mind. By helping others, we are helping ourselves and we build a stronger since of self-worth. As we give, we too receive. The emotional benefit helps us take on life's challenges with purpose, clarity and strength that prevents us from being consumed by the downward spiral of world values.

We promote generosity when we give, because we have witnessed benefits as a society, from working together and being charitable towards the welfare of others. In the case of giving money, the scriptures warn, "The *love* of money is the root of all evil." When we give, it demonstrates that we are free from the ills that are the basis for a lot of evils in our society brought on by greed. A generous heart frees us from a greedy spirit.

We are all susceptible to greed. It brings contention, alienation and a meanness out of people affecting families, marriages, jobs, social and personal relations. Unlike greed, which is like a cancer that eats at the heart, giving frees us from frustrating lives and gives us meaningful relationships and positive influences. We are rewarded in many ways while experiencing an inner freedom and fulfilment of the desire to be good. Giving is a heart regulator.

Including others in our lives brings great happiness. We know how unhealthy loneliness is, especially for someone who is already ill or lives alone. Giving time to others rewards us in the sense that brings us to the conclusion that we have done something right. As noted in the song, "No Man Is an Island," "No Man Is An Island," we connect with others by stepping into their world. We validate their existence and importance to us and receive appreciation, confirming that we are significant in their lives. It's a win-win situation because both the giver and the receiver are deeply appreciative of kindness or benefits received. The core value of sharing time supports the idea that we know what is truly important in life. When we utilize our time well, we experience a sense of well-being.

Whether it is family, church, school or business, we contribute to the greater value of the good by sharing our talents. By nature, talents are meant to be shared. Sharing talents ignite connections in the brain that releases feelings of comfort and confirms the benefit of positive intrinsic and extrinsic exchanges for the experience. As a musician, I am awestruck at the countless encounters when people approach me to thank me for how they connected to a song I sang, the quality of my voice, or the melodic delivery of the text and how it affected them emotionally. It emotionally affected them.

The reason we give is because people have given to us. Everything we are socially, physically, spiritually and otherwise are deposits of people who have invested in our lives from the day we were born. When we become givers, we are demonstrating the dividends of those investments.

DEBRA REED

[Contest Finalist]

Why give? This is a question that is asked by two groups of people. The first is the group with enough surplus, and a heart to help someone else. Maybe these folks have come from nothing and are now "something." So they remember, and never forget to give back.

The other group of persons who think about the question, "Why give?" are those who need. They may have been givers, but are now down on their luck, or they may have always struggled to live from day-to-day. These folks would say without hesitation, "Please give!" They're grateful for any generosity showed to them, and if they have kids, they are doubly grateful.

As a wife, mother, pastor and friend of many, I view giving as reflecting the abundance of life. When I sat and really thought about why I give, it came to me that giving is about life. It's about being a role model and understanding what true success is. It's honoring God's repeated call for us to always remember the poor, and in doing so, we are remembering Him.

The Word of God tells and shows us by examples that it is better to give than to receive. The main word in that scripture is "better." Life is better when you give. If you ask anybody what he or she wants out of life, you will hear, "I want better." But if they understood that feeling better and doing better are directly correlated to giving, they might not be reluctant to give.

The act of giving makes you feel as though you have accomplished what life is all about. Giving provides an opportunity to look beyond our own small world and see the big picture. The big picture is that giving brings life, hope, strength and compassion to the giver and the receiver.

John 3:16 in the King James Version of the Holy Bible says, "For God so loved the World that he gave his only begotten son and whosoever believeth, shall have everlasting life." Jesus gave his life! Because He gave his life, he brought us a better life on earth if we believe in the Holy Spirit, and He assures us a better life after we leave this earth. We have a heavenly home free of everything except pure good. We just need to believe to receive.

One more point! I have learned to never give to expect a return, but give to plant a seed of return. "...for whatsoever a man soweth, that shall he also reap." [Galatians 6:7 KJV]

I've received abundantly from unexpected sources after giving, or sowing where I was led to sow. And my surprise return most often exceeded my gift!

In conclusion, when you give, give from your heart because you believe in everything I've stated above. When you give from this mindset, it will always come back to you "...pressed down, and shaken together, and running over, shall men give into your bosom." [Luke 6:38 KJV]

FAYE SAXON HORTON

[Contest Finalist]

When this question is asked, I am reminded of a conversation between my brother and me. We always wanted to go play with the kids in the alley. However, there were times when our parents did not want us to "go play with the kids in "The Alley". This one time we were told not to leave our own sandy Florida, yet spacious, backyard. I asked my brother why. His reply was, "Daddy said it".

If Daddy said it, it was law. If Daddy said it, it is the word. If Daddy said it, you "had best obey". If Daddy said it, like when E.F. Hutton spoke, you listened. If Daddy said it, even Mama was overruled. You get the point.

The answer to the question, "Why Give?" is because God said it. God is our heavenly and earthly Father. It is He who made us in His image of giving, loving and sharing. It is God Almighty who created us to be like Him. Starting at the beginning of the Bible, the Old Testament, instructions are laid out for giving. Jesus continues instructions for giving in the New Testament. Paul carries the Word of Jesus forward by preaching and teaching the churches about the importance of giving.

Jesus expects and requires all believers to give. Look closely at Matthew 6:2 (NIV): *"So <u>when</u> you give to the needy, do not announce it with trumpets, as the hypocrites do in the synagogues and on the streets, to be honored by others. Truly I tell you, they have received their reward in full."*

Jesus is saying "when" you give, not "if" you give. This, like the choice of playing in our yard or playing outside our yard, was determined by the Father. Jesus is not asking you to give. He teaches what happens "when" you give. Therefore, the assumption is that you will give.

God has given you much so that you can give to others. Why give? Give so that the abundance of God will continue to be given to you. In 2 Corinthians 9:6 (NIV) the Bible tells us: *"Remember this: Whoever sows sparingly will also reap sparingly, and whoever sows generously will also reap generously."*

Jesus tells in Matthew 26:11, there will always be poor among us. Since Jesus told us there will be poor, do you not think his instructions for giving has something to do with the outcome for the poor and the outcome for you?

Three good reasons why you should give:

- Jesus expects us to give and He rewards those who cheerfully give.
- Charitable giving is God's plan* for their survival and your abundance.
- Giving for the right reasons is worship to God.

*Confession from the book "10 Day Study of Prosperity: God's Plan for Success":

> *"I believe and accept the promises of God. God has promised to provide enough for*
>
> *me so that I will be a cheerful and generous giver to His people. I pray in Jesus' name."*

The basics of guidance during our play days continue throughout life. Listen to the Father, heed his Word, and follow His instructions. Why give? Because God said it!

DALE SLONGWHITE

[Contest Judge]

We moved to E. 47th Street. My father read the note taped on the door of the apartment he'd left that morning to attend elementary school. Neither his mother nor his stepfather had mentioned anything about moving at breakfast, but he wasn't surprised. This had happened before, so he walked back down three flights of stairs and slogged three blocks east and two blocks north, searching for his new home.

By the time he left his family back in New York City to join the Navy at the age of 18, my father had lived in 27 apartments/tenements/houses. He remembers standing in line at soup kitchens for a meal, wearing a coat with one arm burned off picked out at the Salvation Army, and beat up if he dared wander off the particular street he lived on into gang territory a block over.

Eventually he was stationed at the submarine base in Groton, Connecticut, met and married my mother at the age of 20, bought a house, and started a business. They lived in three different houses in the same small town until they were 80. But he never forgot the years that molded him and the individuals who reached over the gulf to draw him up from poverty, hopelessness, and a loveless childhood. So I grew up in a home where giving was a priority, an expectation, just something everyone did, didn't they? We never asked why.

I was not raised in a wealthy home, just one with an abundance of love and an understanding of the importance of relationship. We ate supper together every night at 5:00 and shared the stories of our day. We went to the beach most weekends in the short Connecticut summer, all squished on one blanket, no one wanting to be far from the action. We started the school year with three new outfits, nothing added until Christmas along with a few toys.

What we had, we shared with each other and with those around us who were lacking in love, hope, and human connection.

The week before Thanksgiving, we distributed food baskets to poor families. Mr. and Mrs. Peck looked forward to their Thanksgiving basket and the visit each year. Mr. Peck was blind, and they lived in a ramshackle house on the edge of town. The steps leading to the house were splintered and creaky. Their yard was littered with broken down cars, washing machines, and a few live chickens. When my parents moved to Florida in their 8th decade of life, my sister continued the tradition of putting together the basket and delivering it to the Pecks.

Once a week, my dad volunteered in a community service center distributing clothes to the homeless, and once a year, he drove us into New York to peruse a few of his old neighborhoods. Men warmed their hands over fires in barrels, and we offered them bananas from the car window. We returned home with a new appreciation of what we had and what we had to give.

In the last few months of his life, Dad was dependent on a walker or a wheelchair. He lived with my sister Sandy and her husband Eric, and he occasionally fell out of bed. One morning, Eric found him on the floor with a bloodied lip where he'd hit the dresser on his fall. Later on, Sandy brought him to a Bible discussion group she taught where the topic was *giving*. She said to the class, "If you are in a time of your life where you are helping other people, go to the wall on the left. If you are in a time of your life where people are helping you, go to the wall on the right. Or go somewhere in between depending on how you are helping or being helped." We have often laughed at Dad's serious reply, "Wheel me to the wall on the left."

Even to the end, Dad's intention was to help others.

My mother lived by the mantra, *Of whom much is given, much is required,* and she taught it to her four children. "We are the lucky ones," she said. "Poor soul," she would say with compassion about people others might view as being on the fringes of society. She saw them as diamonds in the rough; their glitter she always recognized.

When Mom contracted breast cancer in her eighties, I accompanied her and Dad to weekly chemo treatments. First the weigh in, then the blood test, then the port flushed, then the doctor visit to see if her body could withstand another dose of the poison. If yes, then down the hall to the chemo room with its twelve recliners facing each other in two rows. She nodded at the others hooked up and greeted them with a pleasant, "Good morning," as if meeting them for tea. Dad and I waited while the gruff nurse barely looked up, pointed to Mom's assigned chair, and hooked her up. Never a kind word. Just the grunt of a greeting.

A year passed. A year of my mother's body withering away. One of the last times I entered that chemo room, the nurse raised her head, smiled, and voiced a pleasant greeting. My Dad chuckled as we took our leave. "Did you see that?" he whispered. "That was your mother's project for the last year—to see if she could get that nurse to smile."

Of whom much is given, much is required. Right up to the end.

AUDREY SWIATOCHA
[Contest Finalist]

"I believe that we all have a responsibility to give back. No one becomes successful without lots of hard work, support from others, and a little luck. Giving back creates a virtuous cycle that makes everyone more successful." -Ron Conway

It is an almost universally acknowledged truth that giving of yourself is better than receiving. Scientific studies have shown that giving can alleviate depression and improve physical well-being in people. Businesses have also reported a decrease in employee turnover, improved brand recognition, and attracting better investors. However, these are selfish reasons to give.

To truly understand why giving is better than receiving, one must look at the macro- and micro-chain reactions of being generous. If you perform an internet search for "pay-it-forward streak," you will find several results of people paying for the refreshments of the next customer. One streak in Florida had around 900 participants. One person's act of generosity inspired hundreds of people to behave in kind. Giving results in more giving.

The reason why being generous can be so contagious is because of what it does for the recipient. Giving and receiving is a relationship. You can't have one without the other. In fact, arguing that "giving is better than receiving" only differs from "receiving is better than giving" based on a person's circumstance in life at that moment.

This world tells us that if you work hard, you will get what you deserve. However, this world isn't built on fairness. Equality is still a daily fight for those brave enough to undertake the task and those who have no choice but to demand it. When people talk about obtaining success through hard work, they don't consider the fact that not everyone who seems successful worked hard, and not everyone who works hard achieves success. When your worth is measured by your status and the wealth you've acquired, it's implied that those without are undeserving. When you feel like you don't deserve success, you have very little confidence. Without confidence, you feel powerless to effect change. I know I sure did, but then I made a friend named Oliver.

In 2012 my now ex-husband left me. It was a shock to me because I didn't know my marriage was in trouble. I had a terrible boss, who was also my mom. Our relationship was toxic and she was abusive. Enter Oliver. He kept me company on the phone, video chatting late at night. I didn't even have the confidence to look at his face on the screen. He spent most of the time staring at the top of my head. Over the weeks and months, he built me up. I started making more friends who also worked to build me up. A year and a half after my ex-husband left, I returned to school. I was so scared that the confidence I had to take that step was built on a Styrofoam foundation. I did well, however, well enough to get into my dream university.

I've run across several speed bumps along the way, but I hit one built like a brick wall last semester. I couldn't afford my car payments and my car was about to be repossessed. Anytime I heard a noise outside, I would peek out the window to see if it was the wrecker driving off with my car. I couldn't make the 50 mile trip to class every day without a car. I felt so hopeless, I kept asking myself "why don't I just give up?" My answer was always immediate, "because I can't."

I messaged my friend, Oliver, asking him to tell me something good, something to take my mind off of my hopeless situation. He told me that I could get through this since I had been through worse. He recounted every horror from my past that I had shared with him. I told him that the things from my past might be worse by his definition, but they weren't by mine. Going to school gave me hope for a better life for me and my son. I also felt "at home" there, which is a feeling I've craved for over 20 years. Without a car, I would have to abandon the path that taught me happiness isn't just about not being sad, happiness is an emotion entirely unto itself. Oliver saved my car that day, but he didn't stop there. After saving my car, Oliver got to work raising money on my behalf. He put his talent for sales to good use and raised enough money to prepay several car payments. He raised so much over his goal, he was able to help another family in need.

Several people have helped me along the way, but Oliver stands out because he gave me his time in the beginning. He made me a firm believer in Santa when he gave my son gifts for Christmas. He was my hero in my moment of need. I can easily give him credit for the profound changes in my life. He hasn't had this kind of impact on just me and my son, he has helped several people similarly. If half the people he's helped, help others in similar circumstances, the lives that will be improved will grow exponentially. Since giving inspires giving, my dream isn't just to become an engineer anymore, my dream includes being able to give someone else the priceless gift of feeling like they matter and that there's always a reason for hope.

NOLA WILLIAMS
[Contest Finalist]

Precious people of God, I invite you to take this awesome journey with me in exploring a few perspectives on giving and what it means to me. I do not know when the end of time will come, but I do know that now is the time to allow the Lord God Almighty to use me as a vessel, an instrument here on earth; so that He will be glorified.

My Heavenly Father is the greatest giver there has ever been or ever will be.

The first thing to understand about the question "Why give?" is that giving is an expression of love. Unconditional love caused our Heavenly Father to give His Son Jesus (the greatest gift) for the sins of the world, and the gift just keeps on giving. *"For God so [greatly] loved and dearly prized the world, that He [even] gave His [One and] only begotten Son, so that whoever believes and trusts in Him [as Savior] shall not perish, but have eternal life."* [John 3:16 AMP]

Bless the Lord! Look what you and I have because God gave. *"Love never fails [it never fades nor ends]..."* [1 Corinthians 13:8 AMP] When we live in love we won't hesitate to give.

I know the purpose and plans for my life and the mission that God has placed before me. Giving of myself is at the top of the list. I look forward to the future. It gives me great expectation and much joy to know that Father God loves me and is using me to glorify His name. I am grateful for the Holy Spirit who gives revelation and impartation. Without Him, none of us would be able to do what we do in giving.

He is my helper and support, I don't know what I would do without

His wisdom and guidance in my life. He reminds me of my time and helps me focus so that I won't forget to seek the best and higher good for others.

It is a wonderful thing to make people feel special and important because we are so precious to the Lord. You and I were created to give, to be caring and compassionate, thoughtful, kind gentle and obedient. Let's not forget that being a gracious giver reaps benefits and finds favor with God. This is part of why I give and volunteer to go into the nursing home with the River of Life Christian Center ministry team on a monthly basis. We read scriptures, go room-to-room praying with residents and holding services with them. This is very rewarding. I also enjoy being a volunteer in the God's Anointed Prayer Warriors Ministry (GAP) where we intercede on behalf of God's creation, the church, the world and so forth. Prayer makes a difference and prayer changes things. The

Word of God conceived in the heart, formed by the tongue and spoken out of the mouth is creative power. When we say and pray what God says in His Word the atmosphere, situations and circumstances change. I believe this, so I give.

People of God, we should always give of ourselves, our time, talents and give financially because these are acts and expressions of Worship unto the Lord. These should be exciting times and come naturally that we just do it! Generously giving is important to God; it matters to Him that we be faithful and obedient. *"Now [remember] this: he who sows sparingly will also reap sparingly, and he who sows generously [that blessings may come to others] will also reap generously [and be blessed]. Let each one give [thoughtfully and with purpose] just as he has decided in his heart, not grudgingly or under compulsion, for God loves a cheerful giver [and delights in the one whose heart is in his gift].* [2 Corinthians 9:6-7 AMP]

Listen, we are the Church, the Bride of Christ, and when it comes to our finances I believe we are to give tithes and offerings to the work of the Kingdom of God. This is a vital part of life as a Christian. In fact, it is our responsibility to

give. It is a part of ministry. Without human hands, feet, and vocal cords to speak, ministry would not go forth. I like giving a hug, speaking a word of life into someone's heart, praying a promise for someone from God's Word. These are loving and tender ways to show The Lord's compassion to hurting people on the earth. *"Then saith he unto his disciples, The harvest truly is plenteous, but the labourers are few;"* [Matthew 9:37 KJV]

So let's continue giving of ourselves to prayer and fasting and the ministering of the Word of God so that none of His creation will be missing or lacking anything. Jesus also said, *"...It is more blessed to give than to receive."* [Acts 20:35 KJV] Amen!

Precious people of God, there is power in giving. Why give? Why not give? Selah!

OTIS WINDHAM

[Contest Judge]

Giving may be the key to helping us master some of the ills that plague our lives as human beings. If one observes his/her own actions and how they relate to their life satisfaction, the act of giving adds much to our daily mental and spiritual well-being.

If we think for just a minute, most of us will realize we gain much more spiritually from giving than we do from receiving. This fact is truly brought home when we are able to see the benefit and result of our giving. If giving five dollars allows a homeless person to enjoy a fast food meal or if we just offer an encouraging word to a despondent friend or colleague and see, their spirits lifted, we feel better inside. The amount of joy our hearts receive in helping to relieve another's suffering and increasing their life satisfaction is surely felt even though its magnitude can never be truly measured.

Giving can a multifaceted act. In its purest forms, it can be monetary or financial, material and spiritual. This act can be also be carried out through the benevolence of one's time, knowledge, and advice.

Giving advice, when requested, can be a two edged sword. To provide advice, without expert knowledge or experience, could be a deceitful, ignorant, or duplicitous act. Advice should be given from the heart with no hidden agenda. Offering advice or giving advice out of love and respect from a place of one's best available knowledge and experience is the essence of true giving in this form.

There are many times when money or financial remuneration is the only solution to a perceived problem. It is the responsibility of the giver to be comfortable in providing resources in this method of giving without jeopardizing his/her own personal financial and life-sustaining needs.

I believe, of all the gifts that one can give, those that are not monetary or financial are the most valuable. Knowledge is a great gift when it is given and nothing is asked in return. The *"Give a man a fish and feed him for a day or teach him how to fish and feed him for a lifetime"* adage appropriately illustrates this point.

One can seek and maybe find the knowledge they are seeking using their own means, but how long would it take? To provide a person the benefit of one's knowledge without reciprocity of compensation is indeed a precious gift.

Giving is also spiritual when we give our blessings to the decisions others, in our sphere of influence, have made without our interference. In giving spiritual blessings, we show support and help build the confidence and character of those to whom we give our blessing.

Our gift of our *"Time"* may be the greatest offering we can give. Our time is finite. It is the most valuable asset any of us have as individuals since we as Human Beings have the ability to see an eventual completion of our personal life journey. When we give someone or something our *"Time"*, we have given a most valuable gift.

Giving provides great benefit to the giver. It helps the giver's heart find peace in knowing they have made their fellow man's burden somewhat lighter through this special act of love.

ABOUT THE WRITERS

MARITZA AROCHO-MACDONALD graduated from New York School of Printing High School and attended Brooklyn College. She relocated to South Florida nearly 30 years ago. God has gifted her with the ability to speak and pray with people touching them to know God is the forgiver and provider. For more than 20 years she's served in management roles with her current employer Cooking and sharing with family and friends are her guilty pleasures. She resides in Fort Lauderdale, Florida with her husband Matt.
maritzaarocho@gmail.com

DR. RUTH BASKERVILLE (affectionately called "Dr. Ruth") earned a B. A. in Secondary English, and M. A. and Ed. D. in Educational Administration. She held Principal and Chief School Administrator certification in New Jersey, Florida and Georgia, and enjoyed 42 years in public school education, serving as a high school English and theatre teacher. Besides being the published author of HOODLESS KLAN, FINDING HUMOR IN GRIEF and BEAUTY FOR ASHES: MOURNING TO MORNING, Dr. Ruth is an editor and ghost writer, grant writer, and tutor. When she's not working, Dr. Ruth spends quality time with her daughter, son-in-law and four grandchildren.
www.ruthbaskerville.com

GWEN BENNETT grew up in the inner city of Philadelphia. From humble beginnings, she developed survival skills and the ability to continually re-invent herself. After relocating to Florida, she became a serial entrepreneur; building businesses from the ground floor to grossing millions over the decades. She believes successful business transactions are when everybody involved wins.
gbenn2004@gmail.COM

NANCY FRYE BERGERON lives on the Seacoast of New Hampshire with her husband Jim. They have one daughter, Wendy, who is a high school teacher. Nancy has a blog, [**seacoastwords.wordpress.com**], where she loves to share short stories and poetry with a seacoast theme. Now that she is retired she has more time to work on her biographical novel about her maternal grandmother.
jn-bergeron@hotmail.com

DR. BISHOP WILLIAM CHERRY, JR. is God's visionary for Christ Transforming Ministries (CTM) located in North Prince George, Virginia. He has a profound approach to delivering the Word of God that keeps you coming back with anticipation. His ministry focus is scripturally-based from Romans 12:1-2 "I beseech you therefore, brethren, by the mercies of God, that ye present your bodies a living sacrifice, holy, acceptable unto God, [which is] your reasonable service. 2 And be not conformed to this world: but be ye transformed by the renewing of your mind that ye may prove what [is] that good, and acceptable, and perfect, will of God." He believes that God's Word, when applied, will transform you into the victorious sons and daughters.
Ctransforming@gmail.com

SUSAN M. CLABAUGH lives in Missouri. She is an author and writer who has published articles with Lifeway (Facts and Trends.net) and CBN.com. She also won third place for her children's story at the Heart of America Christian Writer's Conference. Currently, she writes a blog entitled, "Restoring the Soul: Meditations for Survivors of Sexual Assault", to encourage others on their journey in healing from sexual abuse and assault. Susan taught elementary school for eleven years and has her Master's degree in teaching. She loves to write, read, sew dresses for girls in Liberia, work in her churches food pantry, and tutor reading students.
susan.m.clabaugh@gmail.com

ADIEN DIAZ is a mother of three children and a grandmother of a beautiful boy. Adien works full time in the Landscaping industry, assuming an administrative role for a local Branch of the Corporation. In 2013, by a special calling from the Lord she started serving in the homeless community by providing hot meals throughout Central Florida by partnering with the Orlando Union Rescue Mission, Tampa Bay area and Charlotte County. Adien knows the Lord has given her a calling and has been diligently working to fulfill her mission.
Adien.Diaz@bellsouth.net

JEMAL FARELL is an Apostle who seeks the heart of God and enters into his presence through worship. His heart is to see the fullness of Christ manifested on earth and in the lives of God's people. Jemal was born and raised in New York City. He and his high school sweet heart Janel have been married now for 25 years and have four lovely children. Jemal is an ex-drug dealer who is delivered and set free and now breaks the chains of bondage by setting the captives free through the power of the Holy Spirit. Jemal is a living testimony of a word that became reality. His motto in life is we were created to live, not just to exist!
jymal01@gmail.com

DARLYN FINCH KUHN is a prolific poet, short-story writer, and novelist who edits the Scribbles literary e-newsletter and produces book trailer videos. Her debut novel, SEWING HOLES, won First Place in the published novella category of the FWA's 2015 Royal Palm Literary Awards. She enjoys speaking at book clubs, high schools, colleges, and writing conferences, and is also a gifted storyteller. Her work has appeared in literary journals, newspapers, magazines and online. Her poems have been featured on Poetic Logic on WMFE-FM, and been read by Garrison Keillor on the Writers Almanac. She was interviewed on World Radio Paris.
www.darlynfinchkuhn.com

LENA FORD is a wife, mother of three, and a resident of Lakeland, Florida. She is an essential oil enthusiast and has an uncanny love for neckties, bowties, and socks. Professionally, she has a career in the Insurance Industry. Her hobbies include, but are not limited to, travelling, writing, Holistic Health, and preserving legacy. She is the Author of SOULCOUSTIC – (Rhythms from my family tree), a collection of poetry, songs, stories, & sermons from five generations; soon to be released. **lenaford74@gmail.com**

AISHA HIGHTOWER-HALL is a native of Dallas, Texas, an Air Force Veteran and a graduate of California Polytechnic University. She is the mother of five children. She currently teaches at the Cedar Hill ISD. She also is a Photographer, motivator, minister, and the author of, "LIVING AN AWESOME LIFE: WHILE WRITING YOUR OBITUARY".
BOUTTIME07@GMAIL.COM

MARLENE HOENIG is a pastor and missionary. Her ministry includes crisis, trauma, stress, abuse and addictions after- care. She also provides Biblical teaching, coaching, healing and prayer. Marlene ministered globally and has traveled to Alaska, Africa, Nicaragua, as well as numerous states across the U.S. She has many spiritual sons and daughters all over the world, and she desires to see young people equipped and trained for the latter rain. Along with individual and group settings, Marlene ministers at employee meetings and conducts prayer and cleansing sessions by walking through homes and businesses, and across lands. **https://cinderellareleased.me**

FRANKIE JOHNSON [known as "VERSATIVITY" due to his creative and versatile nature] is a creative artist. Growing up in the church sparked his interest in music. He first began displaying his poetic and literary skills in middle school. He refined his spoken word artistry and oratory abilities and further enhanced his music and theatrical skills while in college. Frankie is a Florida A&M University graduate with a B.S. Degree in Graphic Design. Currently, he is a Licensed Massage Therapist, living in Atlanta, Georgia and is pursuing the launch of his non-profit organization which aims at inspiring inner city children who are being reared in single parent households.
VERSATIVITYCA@GMAIL.COM

TEATRA JOSEPH is a native of Orlando Florida. She has a strong passion for music and fondly remembers listening to and singing a diverse selection of songs and musical styles with her mother from an early age. Teatra's interest and passion for music coincided with her ability to write poetry, perform in stage plays, and craft short stories and soliloquies. Teatra continued bridging her musical and literary abilities when she entered collage and begin studying digital audio, radio and television production. She has since developed program scripts and co-hosted the Liberating Truth radio broadcast program. Teatra is a lover of God and ministers His Word in various church production formats. Teatra's first book, "FISHING FOR WORDS: A COLLECTION OF PROSETRY" is a collection of poems she has penned over the past 5 years.
TeatraJay@hotmail.com

STEPHEN LANGE was raised in the San Francisco Bay Area, Steve enlisted in the U.S. Marine Corps after high school as a radio operator and was honorably discharged in 1979. He received a BSEE degree from UT Arlington, in 1987. Steve worked as an engineer writing software for antenna and telecommunications systems. Steve is a member of the Gideons International, a Christian businessman's organization that funds and distributes Bibles all over the world. Steve writes a weekly blog on Christian *topics at www.DeliverMyFeet.org. He and his wife, Gilda, have five adult children.* **steve.lange@swlange.net**

RUBY MABRY is a best-selling author, CEO of mental health facilities, thought leader, and empowerment coach. She is also the Founder of Live on Purpose Movement, through which she unites, inspires, and empowers women to live their true purpose in life and in business. In her spare time, she loves to give back, because she is a firm believer that you haven't learned how to live until you learn how to give. **AuthorRubyMabry@gmail.com**

VERONICA NEALY MORRIS is an author, successful entrepreneur, inspirational teacher and motivational speaker. She is also a Certified Life Coach who has an exceptional gift to transform her experiences of her trials. She has written and facilitated many classes on various topics including "The Power of Words", "The Art of Communication" Walking in Your Truth, The issues of Life, Blurred Lines, You are Enough, The Power of I AM ,The Gift of Universal Laws and "The Effects of Abuse". She currently lives in Orlando Florida with her husband Robert L Morris. **VeronicaNealy@yahoo.com**

CONSTANCE HARRIS POITIER is a graduate of Chipley High School, Bethune Cookman University, Florida Atlantic University, Nova Southeastern University and Crossroads Bible Institute. A National Board Certified Teacher, she has worked over forty years in Education as a Music Specialist. She is the author of The Chase Series, a set of five books about her grandson which opens opportunities for parent workshops about teaching children to read. Constance is also an accomplished singer, and the wife of James Poitier, a professor of music at Bethune-Cookman University.
constancepoitier@gmail.com

DEBRA REED is a wife, a mother and a grandmother, an ordained Pastor, Evangelist and Doctor of Divinity. She is the Founder and CEO of Destined for Destiny Women's Institute. She works closely with her husband, Bishop Dr. Tony Reed as the Founder of Truth By Fire International Ministries, Orlando, FL. She received the Woman of Excellence Award from Business Women in Network and the Virtuous Woman Volunteer Award. She is the author of "A PUSH FROM THE PAST, SHAPED AND SHIFTED FOR PURPOSE AND LIFE PRINCIPLES AND PRACTICAL KNOWLEDGE FOR BETTER LIVING".**truthbyfireministries@gmail.com**

FAYE SAXON HORTON was awarded the Elm City Chapter Business and Professional Women's Award and is listed in Who's Who in American Business Women. She graduated Suma Cum Laude, Albertus Magnus College, New Haven, CT, has LOMA I and II certificates in Insurance. In 1986 Faye wrote "How to Start a Maid Service", which will soon be republished. She is also the author of "Decisions of Life—from The Book of Esther", and "10 Day Study of Prosperity—God's Plan for Success". She is a creative communicator and a member of Christian Women Speaks.
Booksbyfaye70@gmail.com

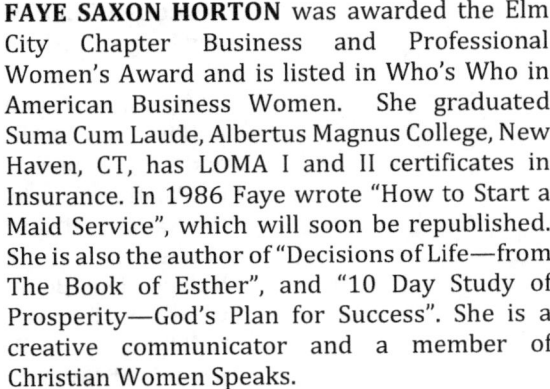

DALE SLONGWHITE founded WriteLines 13 years ago, a business specializing in creative writing workshops and retreats. She is a published author of more than 30 years who writes in various mediums including books, magazines, curriculum, newspapers, newsletters and sermons. Her three latest books are SILENTLY GUIDED: A JOURNEY INTO HEARING LOSS AND DEAF MINISTRY, SAVED FOR SERVICE: THE ARTURO SANTOS STORY, and FED UP: THE HIGH COST OF CHEAP FOOD. Dale is an accomplished speaker and gifted motivator. She conducts creative writing workshops and retreats in Florida and New Hampshire.
www.writelines.net

AUDREY SWIATOCHA has had two consistent passions in life: writing and engineering. After her marriage fell apart in 2012, she found comfort in making friends online. Those friends gave her the confidence and courage to make a radical life change. In March 2015, she returned to school for engineering and discovered along the way that the world is a decent place filled with amazing people. Although she is presented with several challenges as a single parent and full-time student, she can easily say for the first time in her life that she is truly happy.
WickedNerd82@gmail.com

MARCIA WILLIAMS is co-founder of Williams and King Publishers, and serves as the President. She has a passion to see more quality educational, fiction and entertainment publications by African Americans. At Williams and King Publishers, she has spearheaded the publication of various authors, including an offer the National Historic Haitian Center in Miami to publish their Anthology. Marcia is member of Independent Book Publishers Association and volunteers for the Orlando Renaissance Writers Guild. She has a B.A. in Business Management from Oral Roberts University and earned her M.A. degree from Liberty University.
www.williamsandkingpublishers.com

NOLA WILLIAMS is a retiree, who was a dedicated Public Servant 30 plus years. She is an Ordained Elder at the River of Life Christian Center Church and a prayer warrior, encourager, psalmist and writer. God called her Heart to Heart, "A Ministry of Love and Compassion". Her Audiobook "DIVINE HEALING FOR THE ONE I LOVE" is a message of compassion, hope, strength and encouragement for the spirit, soul and body.

ndwhighlyfavored@yahoo.com

OTIS WINDHAM JR. is a native of Laurel, Mississippi and the author of "THOMPSONVILLE COLLECTION: MYSTIC SONG OF THE DEEP SOUTH" and "THOMPSONVILLE HERITAGE: A MYSTIC LEGACY". He serves as an Advisory Board member for African American Golfer's Digest magazine and also a Freelance Travel Writer, and professional Book Reviewer. He serves as Vice President of the Orlando Renaissance Writer's Guild. His interest in writing began as a Freshman in college, and his favorite authors are Cleveland Payne, Walter Mosley, and Stephen King. He is an alumni of Jackson State University, University Southern Mississippi and a graduate of Chapman University.

http://otiswindham2002.wixsite.com /otiswindham

ABOUT THE EDITOR

JILL-CAPRI SIMMS is CEO of Plumb Line Consulting, LLC (a specialized HR firm and the umbrella organization for her literary and media entities). She is also licensed minister and broadcast media host.

The **Authors' Showcase** was launched as a platform for published writers and authors to present their literary work and share their literary journey. The Authors' Showcase provides a learning forum, as well as training and development program for aspiring and published writers and authors to refine their skills, network, and sell their literature via the Showcase book fair.

The essay contest and scholarship program entitled "Why Write?" was launched for elementary, middle, and high school students. The "Why Give?" essay/poetry contest for adults followed suit. She is also a book coach and consultant and guides aspiring and evolving writers and authors through a customized strategic process to aid her clients through the evolution of their book business.

Jill obtained her Broadcast Journalism degree from Syracuse University, Masters in HR Management from Troy University, and Practical Theology Diploma from International Seminary. She is author of a diversity of literary work including her books "HIM", "I AM" and "So Now What?"

info@plumblineconsultinghr.com
www.plumblineconsultinghr.com
theauthorsshowcase@gmail.com
www.theauthorsshowcase.com